Sail Away

Sail Away

Journeys of a Merchant Seaman

by

Jack Beritzhoff

Stillpoint/Memory

Stillpooint Digital Press
Mill Valley, California

Copyright © 2012, Jack Bertizhoff
All rights reserved.

Published in 2012 by **Stillpoint Digital Press**

No part of this work may be reproduced or transmitted in any form or by any means, electronic or mechanical, including photocopying, recording, or by any information storage and retrieval system, without permission in writing from **Stillpoint Digital Press**.

If you have received this book gratis,
please consider making a donation via PayPal to orders@stillpointdigital.com
To quote from or reprint sections of this book, contact: publisher@stillpointdigital.com

"Let's Face The Music And Dance" by Irving Berlin
© Copyright 1935, 1936 by Irving Berlin
© Copyright Renewed. All Rights Reserved. Reprinted by Permission

All images except those noted below
Copyright © 2012, Jack Beritzhoff.
Images on pp.1, 17, 59, 61, 71 courtesy of US Library of Congress
Image on p. 35 courtesy of US Army
Image on p. 7 courtesy of Australian Natrional Library
(cc) Images by the following are used under
a Creative Commons license:
Marion Doss (p. 33), Felix O/sludgegulper (p. 83), prayitno (p. 91)

ISBN: 978-1475143867

Print layout and ebook design by
David Kudler and Stillpoint Digital Press
StillpointDigital.com

To my mother,
who bravely waited for her three sons
to come home

THE AWAKENING

AFTER ALL THESE YEARS I find myself faced with an epiphany. I have at last set pen to paper in search of words that encompass a plot—a story told for one and all to critique—for good or not. While it is true my endeavors have been simple vignettes not immune to faint appraisal, the very idea of my attempt to enter a world of prose or composition is quite curious at this late stage of my life.

In my youth, during the Second World War and for some years afterward, I traveled the world in the service of the Merchant Marine. The globe offered itself as a canvas to be covered with sketches, drawings, and glorious paintings. The easel, oils, and brushes were all there. Sorrowfully, they were never used. I even failed to keep a journal of my wanderings. Light hearted letters to family and friends to temper their boredom were all I had to offer.

The faint of heart, at some point in their lives, are faced with a challenge to fill a void in an otherwise complacent, quiet existence. It is true the art of conversation had never completely eluded me, however stretching it to the written page would be worth an invitation—why not accept the challenge?

As I timidly began my journalistic journey, I found my endeavor had become less burdensome as I slowly recalled memories of my seafaring escapades. To live again all but forgotten adventures, brought forth a youthful vigor that had been lost. As I completed a sentence or paragraph, I found myself gazing off toward a horizon that I had imagined had long ago dis-

Sail Away

appeared. People and places came alive. I was writing of them before it would be too late, before they would have forever vanished in a fog of old age and mental decline. For me it was an awakening.

As to their value, whether my quest results in success or failure, my scenic tales from the road I traveled consumed the need in me to shed for a time the monotonous beat of one's every day existence. It has broadened my newly found knowledge of the independence and fulfillment enjoyed by creators and artists in their search for an aesthetic world. If only for the writing or reading of my simple vignettes, I too, do perceive their intent and wish to join them in my own modest fashion.

From a poet long dead to today's artist:

> *I care not if you bridge the seas,*
> *Or ride secure the cruel sky,*
> *Or build consummate palaces*
> *Of metal or of masonry.*
>
> *But have you wine and music still,*
>   *And statues and a bright-eyed love,*
>   *And foolish thoughts of good and ill,*
>   *And prayers to them who sit above?*

Since I can never see your face,
And never shake you by the hand,
*   I send my soul through time and space*
To greet you. You will understand.
—James Elroy Flecker

Across the
South Pacific

1943–1944

WHATEVER HAPPENED TO IRIS DURANT?

It seems so long ago, that winter of 1943. The place was Newcastle, Australia. The war in the Pacific raged on and most of Australia's stalwart fighting men had been pulled from North Africa and sent on to New Guinea to bolster the line against the

Japs. The absence of many male torsos was evident throughout the area when the American Merchant Ship the Barbara C, pulled into the harbor a few scant weeks before Christmas. We had come to take on a cargo of eucalyptus logs bound for the shallow harbors of New Guinea and the various islands. Our lumber schooner was of shallow draft and perfect for such jobs.

Our ship was out of San Francisco and it had been a long time arriving at Newcastle due to breakdowns, engine problems, and assorted aches and pains. We had stopped in Honolulu; Pago Pago in American Samoa; and Noumea, New Caledonia—delays due to the ship being old—before we had been able to deposit our cargo of lumber in Sydney.

The Barbara C was a steam schooner dating from the 1890's. The schooners were mostly of wooden construction with prominent masts and shallow drafts. Ships of this type had been prevalent in the early part of the twentieth century, running along the Pacific Coast picking up and discharging lumber at various ports from Southern California to the Oregon and Washington shores.

It does not seem so important now who we all were, how we had gotten there and where we were going. We were all in our late teens and early twenties—raised in the heart of the Depression and the War seemed to offer sailing to far away places, a welcome respite from the humdrum pace of everyday life. To those of us with more vivid imaginations, it conjured up shades of high-blown adventure.

Newcastle, named after the more famous coaling city in England, was a small rather colorless town a hundred miles or so north of Sydney. There was a Red Cross Club housed in the downtown area. Loading our ship was a rather slow process, and after standing our watches, we seemed to have plenty of time to frequent the Club and spread our respective enthusiastic charms among the Aussie girls who gathered there. In town there always was plenty of Anzac beer to be drunk in the many pubs, and this fact, coupled with our youthful Yankee exuberance, undoubtedly raised many an eyebrow.

Even though this was a rugged coal-mining district, we Yanks seemed to have gathered a somewhat tawdry reputation. We really could not be blamed for raising a bit of hell, as our voyage over had been one of long and dreary days at sea .

But what of Iris Durant?

She was one of many young and impressionable Newcastle girls who frequented the Club to meet and fraternize with the visiting American youths. They helped serve coffee, food, and various beverages as well as dancing in the evenings to the records of Tommy Dorsey, Artie Shaw, Harry James, and listening to the crooning of Bing Crosby and Frank Sinatra. When the festivities were concluded for the evening, most of the girls usually went to their respective homes, as they were young, unsophisticated offspring of provincial families living in a small coal-mining town, such as Newcastle.

Iris, the daughter of just such a family, was a regular at the Club and loved to dance. She was no more than seventeen, with straw-colored hair and a creamy complexion. She had grey-green eyes and long, slender legs and possessed great body movement. There was an edge to her sensuality that bordered on the expectant.

It always happened that Iris and I ended up together during the last dance of the night.

And so it was, so many years ago, that we were, as the saying goes, so fully taken with each other. We seemed to be waiting for something excitingly romantic to happen—and it very well could with, of all people, a young American seaman off a small obscure Yankee ship. We sensed that we alone of all the dancers on the floor were in possession of a very special kind of ardor and intimacy. We had not yet learned to be hedonistic and I suppose the pure pleasure of this expectancy somehow seemed to escape us.

A weekend came and I was off to Sydney, which was about a hundred miles up the coast from Newcastle. Iris asked to go with me and we traveled together by train. I don't remember all of the particulars, but I do remember a scenario passing through my thoughts on our relationship during the journey: It would be one of idyllic charm, blessed with all the romantic trimmings of a screenplay by Noel Coward. I intended for us to capture all the intimacy and sexuality that we had imagined during our relationship.

Sydney in those days was alive, bustling with the winds of war. It reeked of military people of every gender and persuasion —soldiers, sailors, marines —all wondering if their lives would ever be the same again. There was a feeling of living for the day and of forgetting the pasts that seemed so far away.

Through the haze of so many years past comes a memory of a crafty plan I devised for a pristine rendezvous: Two young people would stay at a small hotel in a faraway Australian city on a wartime weekend. We would not be star-crossed lovers of Shakespeare lore, but eager, happy participants in a new affair of the heart. It would be a Sublime Tale—one that would always remain a loving recollection. I remember looking into her eyes. They were so full of excitement, trust, and delightful anticipation.

My design laid out an interesting and well-understood bit of sensuality by the standards of today; however, the social and sexual habits of the 1940's were, to say the least, more conservative, especially if one were raised in the environment that involved Judeo-Christian conscience. Did not Robin leave Maid Marian for the Crusades? He, of course, was following the straight path to goodness to make up for all the loose folly of his youth—to keep the Faith as it were—to do penance and good deeds and to loosen the guilt the Church had always laid on the backs of the Faithful.

What really did happen that fateful weekend? Well, it came to pass with the scene so well set for a dramatic and amorous episode that time did not stand still nor conscience suspend itself and cast away all youthful inhibitions. There was no small hotel—no utopian episode of Casanovian proportions—no carnal tribute to the gods of the flesh.

When the weekend came to a close, we returned to Newcastle. In a few days I set sail for New Guinea. I still remember our goodbye kiss, so quietly soulful and tasting of passion that had been cruelly wasted. I knew I had missed my golden chance. I never saw her again.

And now at this quiet time of my life, far from the maddening pace of creative years, I fmd myself in a swirl of

Sail Away

poignant memory of that winter of 1943. In the end, I will always wonder if she ever did forgive me or was forever relieved that on that memorable weekend that I had seen to it that she stayed at that bastion of safe virtue and respectability, the YWCA.

I wonder what ever happened to Iris Durant?

Though half a score of years are gone,
Spring comes as sharply now as then,
But if we had it all to do
It would be done the same again.

It was a spring that never came;
But we have lived enough to know
That what we never have, remains;
It is the things we have that go.
—Sara Teasdale

THE GIRL ON THE HILL

We had sailed into Noumea, a port in French New Caledonia—a group of islands in the southwestern Pacific. We were sailors aboard the USAT Barbara C, an old lumber schooner out of San Francisco.

Though we were unaware of it at the time, our cargo

The Girl on the Hill

would eventually take us to Sydney. Our stay on Noumea would be rather short. It was late Autumn of 1943.

The harbor of Noumea was crowded with ships of many nations—a sign of preparation for powerful military action to come. Our ship was timeworn and slow traveling, and after spending many days at sea, we looked forward to shore leave on this Polynesian island.

While stopping in briefly at a noisy waterfront bistro with some of my shipmates, I decided on a less boisterous way to spend my time ashore. I had heard of a church, high on a far hill, with a dramatic view of the harbor.

It was named Église St. Jeanne d'Arc. I decided to make the trek. As I made my way along the path, I became aware of the striking beauty on each side of the road. Lush green foliage and coconut palms lined the way.

 Slowly the tumult of the town faded into the stillness of the hillside. Only the chatter of birds and hidden forest animals could be heard. From far off, the barking of a village dog broke the silence. The sound of my steps on the rocky way made the quietness even more noticeable. The road to the church was steep but its way was made less difficult by small, level trails that would come and go off the main route.

I was halfway up the hill when suddenly from a side path appeared the figure of a girl. I felt rather glad to have the loneliness of my stroll broken by her company. Her English was spoken haltingly with a French accent. She, too, was on her way to the church for a visit and showed no reluctance in talking to a stranger and realized at once that I was an American and clearly from one of the ships in the harbor.

We exchanged names. Her name was Rachael. With the suddenness of her arrival I had failed to take ample notice of her appearance. She was dressed in a high colored blouse and skirt and was wearing sandals. Rachael was no more than twenty, Polynesian, with a strong French allure about her. Her accent and her European features gave her away. Her hair was more dark brown than black, and her figure was certainly slim.

When we reached the crest of the hill and gazed in wonder at the dramatic view, I found the church to be smaller than I had expected. It was more of a chapel. The altar was without pretense and the figures of the saints were showing their age. Only the statue of St. Joan, the Maid of Orleans, stood out for all to ponder: a challenge to the Faithful with sword in hand, she cried out that her faith was worth fighting and dying for.

The church was empty except for us. There were a few vigil light candles still flickering that remained from morning mass. After we had both knelt and said a prayer, we sat in the back pew and talked.

Rachael said her mother was Polynesian and her father was a French seaman who had come to the islands—stayed long enough to court and impregnate her mother—sailed away and was never seen again. Later her mother had married a native man, had two more children—two boys. The three children had grown up together but Rachael had always set herself apart—always thinking that she was special and would some day escape to the great outside world of her father.

As she related her story, I could readily see that the blending of the two races had been exceedingly kind to Rachael. The easy way she had engaged me showed that Rachael was no stranger to visitors to the island, nor was her lament on escaping her life there kept from those who would listen. Evidently I was just another sympathetic listener. I told her I felt incapable of offering advice as so far I had done very little with my life. As I talked, she had slowly lowered her head as if in deep thought. In a few seconds she regained her composure and haltingly apologized for pouring out her feelings to a stranger.

When finally we arose from the pew and stepped from the solitude of St. Joan's, we were faced again with the sight below with its great armada of ships readying for war.

Reluctantly we began our descent and walked slowly along the path to delay our leave taking as long as possible. When we reached the trail where she had joined me, we patiently waited for each to speak—to say goodbye.

I remember telling Rachael that perhaps a handsome island lad would steal her heart away and even reminded her of the old adage that looking far away could easily miss that which is so close.

As I spoke, she kept looking down at the road. When her dark misty eyes looked up at me, I saw the world from which I had only just come appear before me. It was a world of long days at sea—of loneliness, and of uncertain life or death. For this one instant, it became a world to which I did not wish to return. All at once I hated the thought of leaving this island and bidding farewell to Rachael. She had become a Lorelei.

The sexuality of our meeting had been evident from the

start but, due to our surroundings—the church and its environment—I had failed to recognize the true excitement of her utter femininity. I had fallen prey to an exotic spell which she wove so skillfully and being alone with her had set alive emotions that had been stilled for so long.

When at last Rachael beckoned me to step closer and I moved to her side, she gently placed her arm around my shoulder, brushed her lips across my cheek and stepped away. In an instant she was gone. I watched her disappear around the bend of the path.

As I trudged back down the hill, the sounds of the island became silent. The eagerness and anticipation I had felt when ascending to the church had vanished. The beauty of my surroundings was unappreciated. I was lost in a reverie that had happened too quickly for comprehension. My adventure had been incomplete. It would be left with only a beginning.

My quickened steps were bringing me ever closer to where I belonged—to my ship and shipmates. Soon I could hear the familiar sound of the waterfront with its clamor and raucous excitement. When nearing my ship, the shouts and calls from my fellow sailors welcomed me back from shore leave.

Sail Away

When the old schooner slowly made its way out of the harbor, I turned and gazed back at the hill and the church whose presence would glow to me like a beacon far out to sea.

On the following day, as the ship sailed through the waters of the Southwest Pacific, I recall standing at the rail and gazing skyward at the sight of an albatross, the sea bird whose large wings would hover over outbound ships to accompany them on their journey and then disappear over the horizon~ leaving them to find their way alone.

Watching the great bird in its flight fade away against the rim of the sky, I somehow knew that after war, peace, and time long spent in living, far from the activity of daily life, there would come someday, somewhere the poignant rush of a memory returned—the memory of that day on the island at the Church with the girl on the hill.

We have built houses for Beauty, and costly shrines,
And a throne in all men's view;
But she was far on a hill where the morning shines
And her steps were lost in the dew.
—Laurence Binyon

THE ACTOR

IN THE LATE WINTER OF 1943 the American lumber schooner Barbara C was berthed in Lae, New Guinea. We had brought our cargo of eucalyptus logs for the building of a dock there.

I was a seaman aboard the old tub.

The Actor

One night the Salvation Army invited us to an outdoor movie. Unfortunately, the performance was accompanied by high winds and frequent rain. The audience was a mixed one, consisting of U.S. and Australian Army, and us—Merchant Marine.

In spite of the weather, we all soldiered through the movie as the event was a rare treat for us.

During the show an Aussie GI sitting next to me asked for a U.S. cigarette. At certain intervals we had laughed together at the action on the screen. When the movie was over we made our way to the canteen. I discovered his name was Charles and he in no way looked the type to be called Charley. His rank was private, first class, and his age was close to mine. His appearance was just short of handsome and his demeanor was quite aristocratic. His accent was more British than Aussie.

Charles said that many of those who had signed on with him had been sent to North Africa to fight Rommel. His outfit had been detached to the Pacific Area. Australia had given more than its share to the war effort. I had noticed a shortage of young men when our ship was berthed in Newcastle. I avoided telling Charles we had enjoyed the attention of more than a few of the fairer sex there.

He spoke of his home and life in Sydney. As he spoke I could not help blurting out that I'd spent a memorable night there at Romano's, a popular nightclub. He said it was the favorite of his girlfriend. He laughed when I asked if she had red hair. If so, I had danced with her.

As he talked it did seem odd that two complete strangers sitting in an Army Canteen on a rain-swept, stormy night, at a miserable location in New Guinea, could find so much to talk and laugh about. With no sense of bragging he told of his home life, family, schools, and friends—all pointing to a wealthy environment.

The Actor

Charles told me that he was an only child. He said that his father had plans for Charles to take over the family business, but like so many youths born to wealth, he had other ideas. As we talked, I noticed a far-away look in his eyes. This mystery was settled when Charles excitedly told me of his real ambition: to become an actor. He knew his father would be severely disappointed.

That night as we parted we both expressed the hope that we would meet again; before the week was out, we indeed saw each other again at the Canteen. I delivered some cigarettes that I had promised him, and he shared more stories of his dreams and adventures.

On the day of our sailing, he said that he would be at our gangway to say goodbye. True to his word, as we were preparing to cast off, I spotted him there.

At the same time that he strode up our dock, two Australian Military Police vehicles suddenly pulled up behind him. The MPs jumped out and approached him.

Sail Away

There was a short meeting and Charles joined them in one of the jeeps. They then drove off the pier in the direction of the Army camp. As he entered the vehicle I was certain he had given me a wave of his hand.

I couldn't imagine what he might have done to merit such an escort.

Before the Barbara C finally set sail from Lae, I had to satisfy my curiosity. I tracked down some information from two of his mates: Charles had been wanted by the Sydney police on very serious charges—serious enough for Army Intelligence to trace him as far as New Guinea.

The Australians asked if I had heard the story of his wealthy parents. I nodded, and they laughed, then said that he unloaded that tall tale on everybody.

Laughing, they informed me that he unloaded that tall tale on everybody. He was actually from a small, provincial town outside of Sydney.

As we sailed back to Australia my meeting with Charles still lingered in my thoughts. It was as if every experience he had encountered on life's highway—including his encounters with me—had been merely a dress rehearsal for him, not for any understudy part, but for the leading man role.

Actually, he needed very little thespian training. For now, the London stage had lost a real winner. His performance had been Noel Coward personified, and I thought, *If Charles ever gets out of jail, Lawrence Olivier better apply early for his membership in the Retired Actors' Home.*

> *Under the spreading gooseberry bush*
> *The village burglar lies,*
> *The burglar is a hairy man*
> *With whiskers round his eyes.*
> *He goes to Church on Sundays,*
> *He hears the Parson shout.*
> *He puts a penny in the plate*
> *And takes a shilling out*
> — Anonymous

REQUIEM

ONE DAY IN EARLY JANUARY OF 1944 while my new ship, the USAT Colorado, was preparing to sail from Sydney harbor to somewhere in the South Pacific, I watched white crosses being loaded into one of the ship's holds as part of our cargo. As I slowly strolled along the pier, my whole being suddenly changed from everyday normalcy

Requiem

to cheerless, heavy-hearted depression.

Why was fate so unjust—so kind to some and so cruel to those who were marked for our cargo?

To the lucky ones, the war was an ugly, tiresome interruption—a miracle play with a successful happy ending. To others, a tragedy: a morality play tinged with suffering. And for those who had left life's stage, the curtain call was death.

War's theatre encompassed many performers. Some were leading men, but the majority were cast in supporting roles—spear carriers, all steadily marching toward the end of the performance. For some, life dissolved into eternal rest so quickly after such a brief beginning.

Why should the death song be sung so prematurely? As my steps brought me back to the gangway, I wondered who were these men—those who had been driven into the long sleep that life's end demands—those whose eager plans for the future that would never come—those whose dreams for a life filled with blessings never to be realized?

Who were they—those who were destined to claim the cargo lying in wait for them in the hold of my ship?

Sail Away

Time often claims remembrance of things past but I need no Memorial Day to awaken the memory of those who remain so solemnly silent beneath those wooden symbols. The stillness of the vast green arena where they lie, so hushed and voiceless, is broken only by the brush of the rain or the whispering of the wind. In my mind's eye, I can see them now—the white crosses and stars of David standing toward the light and lifting their banners upward to an endless sky, as if to shelter the valiant who suffer no more, and sleep in peace with eternity.

In yonder island, not to rise,
never to stir forth free,
Far from his folk a dead lad lies
That once was friends with me.
Lie you easy, dream you light,
And sleep you fast for aye;
And luckier may you find the night
Than ever you found the day.
—A.E. Housman

SEBASTIAN

IT WAS A U.S. ARMY HOSPITAL far up north on the northeastern Australian coast, near the outskirts of a small town called Townsville. It was a medical facility receiving many casualties from New Guinea and the islands. It was here where I was sent as a patient early in 1944.

Summer down under was hot!

The hospital was spread out in Quonset-hut fashion. Many times our sleep would be interrupted by the sound of men in severe pain. It seemed the war demanded to be continued even in this haven of mercy.

I had been serving aboard the USAT Colorado as the ship's clerk—or what we called the purser. We had come to Townsville on a voyage to the islands and had anchored in the harbor to take on stores. This task belonged to the chief steward and me.

The day was gray and windy with a heavy swell running when the tug came out to pick us up. The chief steward and I started to climb down the Jacob's ladder to board the tug. The smaller ship rose high on the swell and smashed my leg and foot.

Sail Away

That tug did more than crush my leg that day—it changed my young life. I became a captive of the Army hospital's orthopedic ward for many months. My leg required a series of operations, and months of slow healing—all of the time spent in GI pajamas and on crutches.

One day I could hear hearty laughter coming from the far end of our ward. The center of attention seemed to be a lanky GI singing and deftly maneuvering a tap-dance sequence with very talented feet. He was singing "Buckle Down, Winsocki."

Once he had finished his routine, I shouted out, "Best Foot Forward," the movie that had featured that number.

"Right you are!" he called back, and proceeded to come down to my end of the ward. "Hi, I'm Sebastian," he said and again fired off a tap or two.

I introduced myself and we got down to some serious conversation. He had been brought to the hospital after suffering wounds to his shoulder and arm. He had been there only about two weeks and was quartered in the next ward. An Army second lieutenant, he came from Elizabeth, New Jersey. He was about my age.

I told him about my sea-going career and he kidded me about being the only merchant seaman among all the military troops. When I inquired about his battle injuries, he told me the about a Japanese surprise attack on his squad, and of his luck at his survival.

When I looked at Sebastian, the thought crossed my mind that all of his good-natured frivolity could be a charade. Maybe he was all facade. Under all of that cheer, he might very well be a bit despondent for home or about leaving his outfit in New Guinea.

Even so, I was glad he was the way he was.

We talked about show business—something that neither of us knew very much about. I told him that he was lucky: I had been reduced to GI hospital slippers, while he sported leather-bottomed loafers which he had charmed a sympathetic nurse into procuring for him in Townsville.

As for myself, I certainly needed a little change of scene. There were times when I would look at my cast and crutches and wonder if I would ever again tread the light fantastic as lightly as before. After feeling sorry for myself, I would guiltily observe all the real, heroic military patients. So what if I never won any dance contests?

In the weeks that followed, Sebastian told me that, as he had lived close to New York, he had seen quite a few Broadway shows. He liked the musicals best of all. His mother had seen to it that he took tap-dancing lessons when he was quite young. He hated it at first, but as he grew older he started to enjoy it—and besides, it came in handy at parties and was a great way to meet girls.

Sebastian

Dancing seemed to liven Sebastian's personality. Whenever he got depressed, he would put a record on the phonograph, fire off a few taps, sing out a note or two, and all was well.

At the hospital the Army played many popular records in the recreation room. We never got tired of hearing the likes of Crosby, Sinatra, Harry James, Artie Shaw and Benny Goodman. Whenever Sebastian appeared there, he was always called upon for a few steps and a chorus or two. He would get the same reception upon visiting our ward. He would announce his arrival by singing a couple of lines from a song—"The Lady is a Tramp," perhaps, or "On the Sunny Side of the Street." He would deliver a similar routine whenever he visited his old Army buddies who were hospitalized in other wards.

Throughout the long, hot days of our confinement, we would stroll out around the jungle-like hospital grounds.

Sail Away

Actually, he would stroll; my action was a bit more abbreviated because of the crutches. Sebastian spoke respectfully and lovingly about his parents and sister—but only briefly.

Although Sebastian was very agile, he honestly confessed that his athletic prowess was rather poor. In college he had specialized in school plays, drama, and speech. He was a big fan of New York's baseball Giants, and had attended a few games at the Polo Grounds.

He was tall and slim, with dark good looks and a quick smile that conquered all. As for personality, he had it! In truth, he was not as accomplished a dancer as he was stylish, and his singing voice was more casual than cultivated, but when he presented them together, he was a winner!

We liked a lot of the same things. I too was attracted to one of his big interests. While it is true I knew nothing about show business, I knew enough to know that Fred

Sebastian

Astaire and Ginger Rogers were just about the greatest act to come down the pike in years. I remembered so well watching them do their thing." Whenever I saw a large, secluded mirror, I would execute a few fake steps and gestures. Oh! Those elegant black-and-white dance floors in those swanky hotel settings, when for so many of us seeing a five-dollar bill was a major event!

Sebastian remarked once that we should hang on to our friendship and not lose track of each other. He suggested that, after the war—after we had returned home—we should go off to New York and give the Broadway scene a try. I had to laugh when he said, "You might surprise yourself. You could work behind the scenes, become an agent, write scripts, or even turn into on actor. We could seek out part-time jobs to pay the rent. Let's get all of this done before we get saddled with responsibility."

When the time came for Sebastian to ship home, our ward gave him a party. He graciously took all of the kidding thrust upon him for his many fun performances. We envied him going home before any of us, but felt he deserved it.

He had been our Pied Piper.

After he had gone, I had a strong feeling of emptiness. His time with us at the hospital had blotted out for me the heavy-hearted sadness I felt after leaving my ship behind and losing the free and easy life of a young sailor.

Our plans for New York had raised a question in my mind. I wondered if we really would have gone off together to seek our fortunes on the Great White Way. It reminded me of passengers on a cruise ship who enjoy a fun time together and then, when disembarking the ship, vow to keep in touch… though of course they never do.

Sebastian had been gone two months or so when a letter arrived. It was postmarked Elizabeth, N.J. His sister had addressed it to me. In it she wrote of her brother's

Sebastian

friendship with all of us and of his plans with me. She expressed her sorrow at having to tell us the sad news of Sebastian's death. He had been home only about ten days when he was killed in a highway accident.

I wrote back expressing our shock at hearing her news and attempted to tell her of our great fondness for her brother. I told her how much his jovial ways and personality had added to our humdrum life at the hospital.

In the years that have passed since my wartime Australian accident, my life has encompassed a happy family with a dear wife and children, a fine home, a rewarding career, and memories that have endured and lingered over time. One memory, however, has tarried longer than many others. It belongs to Sebastian.

In my home in the small, village-like town in California where I had lived for many years on a hill high among the trees, on certain winter nights when the wind brushed rain against the windows, I could hear the sound of

Sail Away

water tapping against the glass. It seemed like a call to me as the one to Heathcliff from over the dark moors of Emily Brönte's Yorkshire.

I could almost swear it was Sebastian tapping his happy way through life.

Into my heart an air that kills
From yon far country blows:
What are those blue remembered hills,
What spires, what farms are those?

That is the land of lost content,
I see it shining plain:
The happy highways where I went
And cannot come again.
—A.E. Houseman

THE SAILOR WHO MADE BELIEVE

Like so many children of the 1930s, my youth had been uninterestingly minimal—trapped in the vacuum of the hard times of the Great Depression. The war changed this and opened up a new world.

The Sailor Who Made Believe

In March of 1943, I had joined the U.S. Merchant Marine as an ordinary seaman and had been assigned to the USAT Barbara C, an old lumber schooner out of San Francisco. It was a ship out of another century, and was so much more quixotic than any normal seagoing vessel and so antique as to be almost quaint. It would become the perfect vehicle from which to launch my play.

My story is bereft of harrowing sea battles and torpedo attacks—quite the contrary. Our ship had been kissed off as a Second Hand Rose. We believed our course was noble, but there would be no Bronze Stars or Purple Hearts. We realized there were many young men facing hardships and death at the fighting front. Our future seemed less dangerous. It was the luck of the draw. Robert Louis Stevenson I was not, but my play would become a tale told by a first-time playwright, full of the sound of unfeigned truth but tinged with the fury of imaginative make-believe.

Sail Away

The Honolulu we sailed into was definitely Uniform City, with sailors' white caps hiding forehead and military vehicles hogging attention and space—a Pearl Harbor hangover of large proportions. "Leilani" was somehow not so "Sweet."

As we sailed out just a few days later, I imagined with nostalgic envy a white, peacetime cruise ship slowly slipping into a confetti-littered dock. I imagined white dinner jackets and chic evening gowns, captains' dinners, crisp Panama hats, cocktail time at the Moana Hollywood, stars at the Royal Hawaiian, The Duke acting as the crown prince of Waikiki, and the strings of "Aloha" drifting up from dockside.

But reality said that it was off to sea for us.

Pago Pago in American Samoa was exactly as the writer Somerset Maugham described it in his story of "Rain."

The Sailor Who Made Believe

He had described an island town reached from the open sea by a narrow inlet. High purple mountains framed its background. Tranquil waves washed lazily onto a waiting beach. The harbor showed little interest in what loomed outside in the dark deep waters of the ocean beyond.

The war seemed out of place there.

Maugham's story in my head, I smiled at the mirage of a sarong-clad Dorothy Lamour, of bronze young divers atop the masts of sailboats, of slim island girls with comehither plans, of Sadie Thompson swishing her seductive way to the hotel, of sailing ship sailors at the ready to taste the fruits of the island, and of plantation workers behaving badly in a boisterous saloon.

In Noumea, New Caledonia, which was the main Free French base in the South Pacific, the waterfront bristled with military activity. French Polynesia was alive with the Allied invasion to come.

I could swear I could hear the sexy Gallic tones of Maurice Chevalier over the sounds of the town. From a far off bistro the strains of "*Vive la Compagnie*" met with enthusiastic acclaim.

Brightly dressed gendarmes were on the alert for overly-passionate sailors. The *Tricoleur* was raised as seasoned old Legion veterans took the salute. At sundown, the dramatic strains of the Marseillaise drifted out over a silent audience.

⚓

Sydney seemed sort of like San-Francisco-in-Australia, only with more war. And, of course, "Waltzing Matilda" was upstaging "God Bless America."

School girls on a ferry boat made fun of our old schooner. "What war are *you* fighting in?"

The Sailor Who Made Believe

So many well-dressed military everywhere made my humble attire seem somewhat lacking. Khaki pants and shirt were not going to make it. My uplifting fantasy was about to go into action.

I purchased a pair of gabardine slacks, a military shirt, an Eisenhower green jacket, and topped it off with an Air Force type cap. As I proudly took my act to the street, I began to receive salutes. Genuine truth had set in. Time to remove the gold braid from the cap.

With my appearance considerably upgraded, I checked into Romano's, the best night club in town. Of course, this was where I belonged, with all the swells—at home with handsome Aussie soldiers and mixing with the best Sydney offered in feminine chic. No way was I David Niven, but why not qualify as a tall dark stranger?

My adventuresome boldness frowned on the provincial.

I was drawn to the sophisticate, like an elaborate fan to a

masquerade ball or, certainly, like a lemon to a meringue pie.

The Barbara C was always a solitary figure: alone on an ocean, sailing lazily along on a voyage to somewhere. For all we knew it could have been a voyage to nowhere. Never being part of a convoy meant we were on our own. Because of the ship's age, speed would be wanting, so time was ours to blithely spend.

Ancient Mariners were not in our fo'c'sle, but young comrades definitely were. I recalled *Beau Geste*—the love of brother for brother.

I saw us as the last ones standing atop the desert fort as the Arabic hoards approached. Like the buccaneers of old, we would raise our tankards and drink to the revelry of the night. On some placid evenings, I was certain I had glimpsed through the haze of night the shadowy

The Sailor Who Made Believe

image of a ship. Could it have been that of Sir Francis or perhaps the ill-fated Captain Cook?

The shore leave doings of sailors have oft been told by famous story tellers from Joseph Conrad to Jack London. With my usual poetic fancy I recall at times playing a Romeo that would have made John Barrymore sorry he failed to heed his mother's advice to enter the priesthood; however, there were instances when my make-believe Hollywood dalliances had laid the biggest eggs south of Omelet City—reality, front and center.

⚓

On the first day of our arrival in Newcastle, Australia from a second voyage to New Guinea, a Red Cross girl told me of a ship in Brisbane in need of a clerk (or purser). She'd gotten this information from an Army officer friend. With this news, my imagination took flight—this was right up my alley.

Sail Away

When I requested a discharge from the Barbara C, the captain refused, bellowing, "If anyone gets off this ship, it will be me!" —much to the laughter of the crew.

When night fell, I was off by train to Brisbane, sea bag packed and not without some apprehension. I was Fletcher Christian of the Bounty, ridding himself of a bad situation. As I glanced backward there appeared the figure of *The Scarlet Pimpernel*. Were they seeking me as they did him?

When I reached my new ship, USAT Colorado, I was not exactly piped aboard, but was cordially and thankfully received without question or fanfare. My knack for imagining had suddenly elevated me from ordinary seaman to ship's officer.

⚓

As the year of 1944 was enjoying its infancy, the Colorado lay at anchor in the harbor at Townsville. It was

The Sailor Who Made Believe

there I suffered a severe accident and was confined to the US Army hospital for many months.

My doctor and nurse had become more than friends. With my fondness for the imagined, I had sensed a romance growing between them. During their night rounds, I had heard their intimate musings and was certain their romantic cup was running over. I visualized a *Farewell to Arms* scenario—Gary Cooper and Helen Hayes thrown together by a hospital and war. I saw them at war's end tearfully and joyfully reuniting as the music swelled in the background, supplying a happier ending to the Hemingway tale.

Near the end of that year, some of us were flown from the hospital to Brisbane to board the hospital ship Monterey, whose task it would be to provide a final voyage for us to San Francisco and, for me, home. The curtain had fallen. There were no final bows to be taken. The theatre lights had been dimmed. No bouquets were offered the

Sail Away

actors. There were no plans for road performances.

There was silence in the building. My play was over.

There is a dish to hold the sea,
A brazier to contain the sun,
A compass for the galaxy,
A voice to wake the dead and done.

Imagination, new and strange
    In every age can turn the year;
Can shift the poles and lightly change
    The mood of men, the world's career.
—John Davidson

Over the Seven Seas

1947–1952

A STOLEN SWIM

THE U.S. PACIFIC COMMAND'S RECENT DECISION to declare Guam a "key element of support to U.S. investments in the Asia-Pacific region" brought the memory of the Guam of another day to my attention.

It was about two years after World War II. Our tanker,

A Stolen Swim

the SS Fort Wood, lay at anchor there off the quiet side of the island. We carried a military cargo of oil and were waiting for berthing dock on the island's busy port. The afternoon was hot and humid. From the beach came the sound of happy swimmers. In the distance, we spotted some Army vehicles. Clearly, this was a prized spot—perhaps frequented by the Officer's Club.

Aboard all was quiet and subdued. The old man was probably enjoying a nap. As the third mate, the first assistant engineer and I, the purser, longingly surveyed the site before us, a sudden thought came to all of us at once. There was a rubber pontoon raft handy, just the ticket to lower and row the one hundred yards or so to join the revelers, enjoy a cool swim, and return to the ship with no harm done.

Without so much as a by-your-leave, we lowered the raft and were on our way to share an afternoon swim with our Army hosts.

As we approached the shore, we failed to take notice of a large, treacherous reef sheltering the beach. After many moments of nervous, careful maneuvering, we at last reached our destination. Unfortunately, in the process our raft was badly punctured. Ignoring all foreboding, we happily cast in our lot with the revelers, plunged

Sail Away

into the waves and left the thought of any consequence far from our immediate interest. Finding fraternization no particular problem for us, we immediately hit it off with our newfound hosts.

As the afternoon grew late without our noticing, our newly acquainted comrades gradually disappeared, heading back to their military base. It was then that we at last came face to face with the glaring realization we had been left without a return ticket. The penalty was about to be paid. Marooned as veritable castaways, and wondering what our future lot would be, we slept on the beach that night and were severely attacked by the island's mass of blood-hungry mosquitoes.

That night, lying on the deserted beach, I remember gazing up at stars made bigger by being viewed from the midst of a dark sea.

Only the sound of waves, quieted by the reef, lazily lapping ashore, broke the night's silence. Left in isolation, body still damp, fighting off pesky insects, it seemed no time for deep reflection. Nevertheless, I began to wonder about our impulsive action, and more importantly on my own life.

Why was I still playing the vagabond, forever living a

devil-may-care existence? Why had reality become my foe? Why was I resisting the usual plan for a normal, conventional life?

Time enough to join the struggle of responsible living, to create a family life, and pursue a more meaningful career.

I recall quieting my anxious reverie with the old Irving Berlin lyrics:

> *Before the fiddlers have fled.*
> *Before they ask us to pay the bill*
> *And while we still have the chance.*
> *Let's face the music and dance.*

In the morning we were greeted with the sight of an empty ocean as our ship had up-anchored and departed for the other side of the island to discharge its cargo. As my two shipmates were charged with standing watches, their indiscretions were a serious matter. For myself, the comical side of our adventure came more to the foreground, as I suddenly realized we were in a similar predicament to two sailors in Noel Coward's 1936 musical *Red Peppers*. The drunken sailors overstay their shore leave, and as they face the deserted pier, they shout and sing, "Has anybody seen our ship?"

Sail Away

Eventually, we hitched a ride from a friendly Army jeep whose GIs couldn't resist a laugh at our folly. As we approached the gangway one can only imagine the greeting we received from a red-faced, waiting skipper. His tirade continued all the way through the noon meal. After all, his problem could have been, shall we say, a lot more serious. Although the comparison was more than a bit off the mark, I could not resist thinking that the old man had it rather easy when one considers what William Bligh of the HMS. Bounty faced, greeting his errant sailors returning after many nights of high decadence on Tahiti.

Now that must have been really something!

Better to see your cheek grown hollow,
Better to see your temple worn,
Than to forget to follow, follow,
After the sound of a silver horn.
Better to bind your brow with willow
And follow follow until you die,
Than to sleep with your head on a golden pillow,
Nor lift it up when the hunt goes by.
—Eleanor Wiley

ROSES

IT WAS THE SPRING OF 1948. Our freighter had been tied up in Naples, whose reputation has always been sullied by the prestige of the more famous cities of the north of Italy. Nevertheless, Naples was truly the metropolis of music and Capri-like, carnival ambience—with the common man's relish for the mundane. No dainty appetites here. I can still hear the waiters croon their arias in the local cafes as the patrons join them in their theatrics. Over the years its mischievous reputation has endured to further foster its earthy love of life.

One evening just before midnight—the crew of the John B. Hamilton seemed to be making a long night of it—I was returning from the city, when I noticed a solitary figure standing in the shadows of the dock. As I approached the gangway I could hear the muffled sound of steps approaching me. I turned and saw that it was a woman of advancing age, a black shawl pulled closely around her stooped shoulders to shield her from the cold night air.

She carried a rolled up canvas of some sort beneath her arm. She said it was a painting that she wished to sell. As merchant seamen we were constantly besieged by locals to buy their various items at so-called bargain prices, almost always accompanied by hard-luck stories.

Sail Away

I had made it a rule never to encourage them.

Glancing at the old woman, however, I felt a natural surge of compassion and deemed her worthy of making an exceptionto my rule. I asked her to come aboard for sandwiches and some hot coffee.

Once we settled into the empty mess, I had a good look at her. The toll of years had left their imprint. A long life had dimmed the brightness in her eyes and quick laughter had abandoned her.

When at last she slowly unfolded the canvas there came into the drabness of the room a sudden burst of radiance. It spoke of simple elegance and beauty so in contrast to the harsh realities of the loud and raucous spirit of the city.

The artist had painted roses—no landscape or other figures, only red, pink and white roses in full bloom, spilling out of a blue bowl onto a dark tabletop. Suddenly the room became infused with their glorious fragrance. I was transported.

As I look upon the painting, in my possession still so many years since that night in Naples, I wonder at my heart's surrender to the gossamer, delicate beauty of the roses. Why did I allow that emotional fervor to invade my sensibility? It was almost as if the poets themselves had permitted me entrance to their lyrical world of sonnets and verse—that for that one instant the likes of Percy Bysshe Shelley or Lord Byron himself had bid me welcome into their heroic company.

> *It was a bowl of roses;*
> *There in the light they lay,*
> *Languishing, glorying, glowing*
> *Their life away.*
>
> *And the soul of them rose like a presence,*
> *Into me crept and grew,*
> *And filled me with something - someone ~*
> *O, was it you?*
> —William Ernest Henley

A SECOND LOOK

WORLD WAR II HAD BROUGHT a new awareness to the world's wonders and its tragedies. Those involved found themselves pausing to linger a bit longer at life's treasures.

A Second Look

Their waste would be a sad mistake. *Look now*, we learned, *for fate has no appetite for loitering*. The miracles that are all around us would never again command such short attention.

April of 1948 found my ship, the SS John B. Hamilton, busily discharging cargo in Genoa, Italy. As a member of the crew I had looked forward to visiting the birthplace of Columbus. On shore leave I happened to pass the city's main theatre, where Pucini's opera *La Bohème* was being performed. After looking over the poster and various photos of its performing artists, I resumed my idle wanderings.

I walked on a short distance, and then suddenly paused. My mind wandered back to the opera house.

I had never attended an opera. In fact, I had often scoffed at its loud, melodramatic theatrics. Why not avail myself of this opportunity to see for myself what all the noise — the praise and acclaim — was about?

Sail Away

I decided to turn back and purchase a ticket for the night's performance.

As I sat in the my seat in the old opera house that evening awaiting the curtain's rise, I was well aware of the anxious enthusiasm of the boisterous, expectant audience.

When the opera commenced I found myself a willing and excited patron, challenging the cast to convert me to their magic.

When Giacomo Puccini's melodious score rose from the depth of the orchestra pit and soared, my whole being rose as well, and I was transported to that romantic, sense-rich land to which music can lead. The violins rose up in full flight to match the majesty of the composer's notes. The voices of the performers rang out, powerfully telling the story being played out with all its drama and pathos.

A Second Look

In the end, above all, I remember how the sweep of Puccini's score—pure, earthy, and poignant—evoked such a deep feeling in my heart! How lucky I had been to turn back from my idle wandering to seek admittance to such pleasure.

When I was young, I found myself too caught up in idle distraction to observe the trees desperately clinging to the leaves that were turning to colors, red and gold. The trees, however, somehow sensed that their beauty would soon disappear, as the winds of autumn brought their adornment drifting to the ground. They would face the long winter longing for the spring that would bring a new and welcome dressing to cover their nakedness.

Now, after time spent in the living of a long life, as I feel the wind heralding the autumn of my own year, I linger for an extra moment or two at the sight of those same trees with their bright colored leaves.

Sail Away

I have come to appreciate the true beauty they possess and deem them deserving of a second look before they fall to earth to die.

> *What is this life if, full of care,*
> *We have no time to stand and stare?*
> *No time to see in broad daylight,*
> *Streams full of stars, like skies at night.*
> *No time to turn at Beauty's glance,*
> *And watch her feet, how they can dance.*
> *A poor life this if, full of care,*
> *We have no time to stand and stare.*
> —W.H. Davies

THE KEY

EARLY IN 1948, the SS John B. Hamilton arrived in Casablanca, French Morocco on the shore of the cool Atlantic. On the night of our arrival, having nary a watch to stand since I was purser, I dressed and stepped ashore on my own with no shipmates in sight.

The Key

The evening was young and the air was filled with the fragrance of Casablanca exhilaration. When arriving in port for the first time, I always found myself wondering what lay in wait for me just around the corner. I had developed a fondness for walking down a strange new street. My imagination worked overtime as I looked forward to new people and sights and perhaps a heart stirring adventure that would banish the monotony of shipboard life.

Abandoning the noisy *bistros* near the waterfront, I happened upon a small, cosmopolitan bar in the better section of the city. The place reeked of sophistication.

The girl tending bar matched her surroundings, her smooth good looks mirroring her workplace. I soon learned her name was Simone. Her elegance in the demeanor department coupled with the slick polish of the establishment called for champagne cocktails as my drink of the night.

Sail Away

As the evening progressed, I observed that the bar business was on the quiet side affording me more time to capture Simone's attention and for an intimate conversation.

She had come to Casablanca from a small town many miles away. Her departure had been hastened by a broken engagement. Her appearance and engaging personality had soon gained her employment at the bar. She was evidently enjoying success, as she told me in passing of having her own apartment in the better section of the city. She loved her family and missed them, but was attracted to the more urbane life Casablanca afforded. It was apparent to me that she was much too attractive to be lacking in masculine companionship.

The time I spent with Simone flew by, and before long I considered returning to my ship. I hated the thought of leaving. The night seemed shorter with each libation. Time for one more cocktail.

The Key

Before I had finished my drink, Simone offered her hand as if to say goodbye. In doing so she, slipped a key into the palm of my hand. She then wrote her address on a slip of paper and instructed me to give it to the driver of one of the horse-drawn carriages promenading along the dimly lit streets who would take me to my destination.

Striding along, I laughed to myself as I recalled the movie *Casablanca* with its images of Humphrey Bogart and Ingrid Bergman. The champagne helped, but this was, after all, that same French Moroccan city of intrigue, and I had invaded its world.

When finally arriving at the given address and dismissing my driver, I approached the front door of the apartment, which was on the ground floor. I inserted the key but received no response. After stubbornly trying many times to gain entrance, the excitement of the evening slowly vanished and I was faced with the sudden realization that Simone had either mistakenly given me the wrong key, the wrong address, or was playing a massive trick on me.

I stood silently at the entrance, eyes intent on the front door listening to the vanishing sound of the horse's hoofs as the carriage was slowly disappearing from sight. I can only wonder at the absurd look that must have graced my face. Simone was too discerning and astute to make a mistake. No, the joke was on me. Whether mistake or intent, my winning way had obviously been overrated.

Before the next night had fallen, our ship had sailed and the mystery of the previous evening had been left unsettled.

The key had failed to open the door but it did unlock the entry to my own persona; the mask slipped and revealed a notable ego and rather overblown assessment of my own charm and laid bare my more modest assets.

"How strange the changes from major to minor." The Cole Porter lyric certainly did fit me to a tee.

For what wert thou to me? How shall I say?
The moon, that poured her midnite noon
Upon his wrecking sea,
A sail that for a day
Has cheered the castaway.
—Robert Bridges

A REAL GOOD SMOKE

IT IS HARD FOR ME TO FORGET the Year of our Lord 1949, for most of it was spent on round-trips from Heysham, England on the Irish Sea to a faraway desert outpost: Kuwait, in the Persian Gulf. My shipmates and I had sailed out of Charleston, South Carolina. I served as purser aboard the Merchant Marine tanker, SS Ampac California. Our mission was to quench the everlasting thirst for "Black Gold."

Heysham, a small town in the west of England, would be our home port for the better part of a year. The closest city of any status was Liverpool.

On regular runs we would sail along the coasts of Spain and Portugal, pass through the Strait of Gibraltar and enter the Mediterranean Sea on our journey to Port Said in Egypt and the Suez Canal. This route would take us to the Red Sea and onto the Indian Ocean, finally arriving in Kuwait with its precious treasure of crude oil. The place still remains in my memory as all heat and sand. When our cargo was safely aboard we faced the long journey back to England.

Kuwait, a small country next to the larger Iraq would someday, as we know, loom large on the world's stage when American GI's would fight to protect Arabs from

Sail Away

being destroyed by other Arabs under the command of Sadam Hussein.

Heysham, our other terminus, offered few opportunities for seamen to throw off the long, unvaried days at sea. It was a colorless, drab town with one dance hall. The girls who lay in wait for us were not exactly counting on Hollywood contracts and I don't remember any of them reminding me of Lana Turner.

On one stay there, the crew were discharging our cargo. The third mate and I, seeking to break up the usual monotony, thought up the idea of testing the market for our American cigarettes.

Even though the war was long over, 1949 found British cigarettes still severely rationed. When they could be procured, the public found them much inferior to ours. Whenever we frequented a bar or social setting and lit one up, all eyes would turn towards us, and we were glad to share with the eager Brits.

A Real Good Smoke

Merchant ships carried various items of sundry nature for the benefit of the crew, such as shaving gear, toilet articles, candy, etc.—and most importantly, cigarettes. Once a week the purser (which is to say, me) dispatched these items (for a minimal charge) from a small nook of a space called the slop chest.

With the consent of Captain Hansen, we decided to test the black market in London, and I, as purser, literally possessed the key to such a test. We purchased two full cases of Pall Malls from the chest and contacted a cab driver with a connection in London. It would be an overnight trek with an early-morning arrival.

As we sped through the night—through Manchester, Birmingham and vast countrysides —getting ever closer to our destination, an eerie feeling began to sweep over me. Here we were, arriving in London—one of the most majestic cities of the world—a city that was the center point of the British Empire upon which "the sun never sets." It seemed such a pity to approach it in grey semi-darkness instead of catching its grandeur in the bright light of day.

In the early morning, as we reached the quiet streets, my conscience had awakened to our entrance to such a noble city being steeped in shadows rather than one of more honorable intent. The sun had only just shown itself when our driver pulled into a dark dock area, deep along the Thames—a place that would have made even Sherlock Holmes cast a disapproving eye.

The person in charge of the black market operation was an old woman sitting in a rocking chair—Madame Defarge from *The Tale of Two Cities*. "You are Americans," she slowly uttered, and then asked from what city in America we had come.

I quickly answered "Chicago," thinking perhaps she would be impressed with its identification with Al Capone and gangsters.

A Real Good Smoke

She couldn't have cared less. We got down to business.

When our dealings were completed, for some bold reason I asked for a recount of the pounds she had doled out. I had spotted a shortage in her count. As I glanced at the third mate, I could see the utter terror in his eyes.

When the counting was over and I had been proven correct, she appeared almost impressed by our sheer impudence. Without further fanfare, we took our hasty, nervous departure.

Luck had been with us. We had received a bounty—a treasure, a windfall! We had broken the bank, so to speak. I felt like I was leaving the casino at Monte Carlo. Brave heart had paid off. The pound in those days gave way to a bevy of dollars. But alas, our stay in London town was far too short. It was a pity that I would never see if "the British Museum had lost its charm," as the Gershwin song had declared.

Sail Away

Now, with so much of the past in view, my conscience has slightly healed itself by reflection on the enormity of pleasure we had bestowed upon the tobacco-starved British public—by the genuine thrill of seeing so much money at one time—by the look on the Captain's face—by the pure drama of the retelling of the deed, and lastly, when coming home, the helping hand I had given to my dollar starved younger brother on the occasion of his wedding. The incredible drama of our ruse and our good luck in no way erased the fact that we had chanced a trip to the dock of the Old Bailey, or at least a stay in the local constabulary.

Our lack of respect for the law could not be wiped away by our success. I was definitely not a soldier of fortune; however, I did have a taste for adventure. I was a young, wide-eye sailor, and you know what they say about sailors!

I wonder what King George would have thought about

our deed. I suppose it all depends on how desperate he was for a real good smoke!

I was happier than the larks that nest on the downs and sing
    to the sky —
Over the downs the birds flying
    Were not so happy as I.
It was not you, though you were near,
    Though you were good to hear and see;
It was not earth, it was not heaven,
    It was myself that sang in me.
— Sara Teasdale

PARTY BOY

THE MEXICAN PORT CITY OF ACAPULCO is now one of the most popular resorts in the world. Its warm climate and sultry Pacific Ocean breezes charm even the most discriminating of tourists. But I remember a time when it was only a small undiscovered seaside town....

Party Boy

Near the end of 1949, I found myself performing purser's duties aboard the Coastal Nomad, a small Grace Line motor vessel (a combination passenger and freight ship) on a coffee run down the Pacific Coast to Mexico and Central America. We were to lay at anchor there for only a day and night.

Directly on the beach stood a group of buildings, including a cantina and various living- and ship-related structures, which seemed to please most of the crew allowed shore leave.

As I gazed upward I spotted a building on a hill above the harbor. Upon further inspection—after a stroll from the town—it turned out to be a small residence hotel overlooking the harbor. As I stood on the cliff I could see our ship anchored below. Upon entering the hotel, the shouts of happy laughter told me a party was in full swing around the bar. The participants, as it turned out, were mostly Texans and well-heeled Mexicans. I received a loud and enthusiastic welcome. The party had clearly been underway for quite a while: the participants in no way lacked the high frivolity that accompanies liquid spirits of strong velocity. After a drink or two, I found it much easier to join my new friends in their happy partying.

Naturally, they wondered at the suddenness of my arrival. With an abrupt burst of devil-may-care, I at once upped my life status to that of a writer travelling as a passenger aboard the ship at anchor below the hotel cliff. Upon hearing this news, the guests introduced me to a genuine, real-life author among the group who immediately showed great interest in my background, body of work and general history. My questioner was a young woman of strong literary history and the writer of two successful books on A WOMAN'S QUEST FOR EQUALITY. She seemed to be doing all right in the looks department also....

Party Boy

I finally confessed that I was indeed a novice working on my first novel and lucky to be taken as a passenger aboard the coffee ship. In a more quiet space outside the bar area, we found ourselves in deep conversation. During our talk, I found it quite ridiculous that I, an imposter, was actually engaged in serious discourse with the real thing. I had become an instrument of deception—a fraud and charlatan and, more importantly, I seemed to be enjoying it. Deep inside I wondered if my masquerade was truly as successful as I thought. She smiled at some of my musings, but after sharing another drink, it ceased to be important.

For me, my leave-taking that night was one big letdown. I had found myself caught up in a grand charade which I hated to see end. Nevertheless it entailed the usual goodbyes, the good-luck wishing all around and the final realization that the party was over. To be honest, I had to question what impression I had made on my new found friends.

Sail Away

To my great surprise, the verdict seemed to suggest the affirmative. The next morning when my ship sailed, there they were, on the hill in front of the hotel: waving a fond farewell to a novelist whose fame someday they hoped to recognize.

Tell all the Truth but tell it slant —
Success in Circuit lies
Too bright for our infirm Delight
The Truth's superb surprise

As Lightning to the Children eased
With explanation kind
The Truth must dazzle gradually
Or every man be blind —
—Emily Dickinson

THE SKIPPER

THE CAPTAIN HAD LEFT TROMSO, NORWAY to sail as a cabin boy in the British Merchant Navy. Eventually he became a U.S. citizen and gained his Master's papers in the U.S. Merchant Marine, working for the Union Oil Company as a skilled tanker man. When World War II

The Skipper

began he was accepted into the U.S. Navy and given a commission, assigned to Admiral Halsey's staff directing the refueling of Navy ships at sea.

I first met Captain Ted Hansen in early January of 1947, when I reported for duty as purser aboard the tanker SS Fort Wood in San Francisco. I recall our initial meeting with some chagrin. He had directed me to write and type some correspondence for him and when I had completed the work, I handed it to him. He took the papers from my hand, glanced fleetingly at their contents, and proceeded to toss them onto the deck while uttering a loud and dismissive expletive.

Noticing that he was obviously in a foul mood, I should have given pause before my next move. For some uncanny reason I blurted out: "Captain, in the U.S. Navy you probably had three or four yeoman to do this work for you, but now you have only me. I don't think I should have to pick those papers up."

Sail Away

The startled, stern look remained on his face for a few seconds before he gave out a hearty laugh, uttering, "I really didn't think you had the nerve to say that! " With that, I picked up the papers off the ship's deck.

Over a span of years, on tanker and freighter alike, we sailed together as shipmates, and over time forged a strong and lasting friendship that bridged rank and dissimilar backgrounds. Whenever the Captain took command of a ship, he would ask for me to act as his purser.

I don't believe it was ever my clerical ability that he held in high esteem, but more my ability to make him laugh. Our relationship was like father and son—the son he never had and the father I never knew. Though our personalities were as contrasting as port to starboard, there I would be, striding alongside, attempting to keep step; myself a failure at real seamanship, like a coat with no pockets, redeemed only by an ability to form a coherent sentence and a knack to amuse: a Falstaff to the King!

The Skipper

Captain Hansen had a wife and a grown daughter and a home in San Pedro, California. His spouse seemed happy with her Norwegian Club activities—and luckily so, because her husband's real home was the sea. Over the years we sailed together, countless horizons and sunsets came and went, from the West Coast of California to the Panama Canal, the Caribbean, the East Coast, Persian Gulf, Europe, Taiwan, Hawaii, the Philippines, South Pacific, and finally the Korean War, with a regular run between Sasebo, Japan and Pusan in Korea.

⚓

So many remembrances of the experiences we shared, humorous and dramatic alike: too many to recount in their entirety.

Yet there are some that are set apart and remain most vivid in my mind's eye:

The proud grin from the bridge as he skillfully guided

the vessel alongside the dock for another perfect docking, accompanied by a shout-out to me: "Johnny, how about *that*?"

⚓

The laugh he enjoyed in Heysham, England as our tanker, the Ampac California was pumping oil ashore... and the third mate and I were doing our bit for our British cousins by selling American cigarettes at a fantastic profit.

One night, after an expansive dinner aboard ship, imbued with much brandy and wine, the Captain offered his guest, a high-ranking British Naval officer, a cigar.

The Brit accepted, but then the man proceeded to step out onto the deck to smoke—a literally mortal sin on a oil tanker.

The Skipper

Upon seeing this and remembering the rough life the Skipper had endured in the British Merchant Navy, I wasn't at all surprised when he stepped forward and deftly flicked the cigar from the mouth of the startled officer.

Staring at the Brit's astonished expression, Captain Hansen howled with laughter. "I've waited all my life to do that!" he exclaimed.

⚓

The thrill for me standing alongside him on the bridge as he gave two blasts of the ship's whistle as a salute to my friends standing on the deck of their Telegraph Hill home.

They were waving towels in farewell as we headed out toward the Golden Gate Bridge on a voyage to the Far East. We had shared a party with them the night before.

Sail Away

The good feeling within me when, on the occasion of not having to stand watches, I was often invited into the Captain quarter's after our evening meal to share a drink or two and lively conversation with him as the Ampac California plied its lazy, monotonous way from England to the Persian Gulf.

I can see him now: pipe in mouth, recounting his many sea adventures and escapades with a mixture of joy and remorse.

And, lastly, the memory that still looms large in my mind's eye:

In early January of 1952, in the middle of the Korean War, while the San Mateo Victory was discharging cargo in the harbor of Pusan, Korea, Captain Hansen took gravely ill and was confined to his quarters. Amongst

The Skipper

my duties as a purser was attending to him in his illness, which was unknown to me.

His condition grew steadily worse and after some time we finally signaled for help.

As I remember, it was a bitterly cold night in Korea when he was taken by motor launch to a U.S. Navy hospital ship in the harbor. It has long been in the shelter of my heart, the raw emotion that engulfed me as I watched my friend being separated from his ship, never to return. I was certain he had saluted her, and I knew he had surely mustered a wave of his hand to me.

He was flown to a Navy hospital in the San Francisco Bay Area. The verdict was cancer. The chief mate brought the Skipper's ship home to San Francisco.

Sail Away

Once we arrived back at the port where I had first gone to sea nearly a decade before, I signed off our ship to end at last my own sea-going life.

I visited my old friend in the hospital. As his look of surprise and welcome slipped away, a far-away stare appeared in his eyes. I knew for certain that the memory of our happy times together had shown itself for perhaps a last time.

We shook hands and held on for a few long minutes before letting go.

He died soon after.

As the years have quietly drifted away, I have, at times, recalled when I was once a sea rover, an oceanic wanderer, a vagabond without care—a sailor in the Merchant Marine, who could leave far behind the worries of the world. Today, the roar of the wind's fury and the sound of the sea's song are all but forgotten and what remains is the rush of the happy times on board ship and ashore with shipmates.

Of the many sailors I encountered during my years at sea, there was one who shines brighter in memory, as he had a most significant impact on me. He was the Skipper, who will forever command from me a salute and a salvo of deep respect, accompanied by a warm affection.

Whatever my colors, I dip them to you, Captain Ted Hansen.

To me, fair friend, you never can be old,
For as you were when first your eye I eyed,
Such seems your beauty still.
—William Shakespeare

WHEN THE MUSIC COMES IN

Where does one begin about an ending?

My sailing days came to a conclusion on February 28, 1952 in San Francisco. I signed off my ship for the last time. She was the San Mateo Victory and we had just

When the Music Comes In

returned from Korea.

On that day, as I walked away from the pier, I remember staring a little longer than usual at her.

As a movie fan, I had always been impressed by the soft, poignant music that drifted into the background of a scene to enhance the drama of the moment. I could feel this happening to me as I took a last look at the ship—*my* ship—that had safely carried me home from a distant land.

It was more than leaving the sea behind; it was the arrival of a new day for me. I was finally facing the world as it really exists.

Gone forever would be carefree, irresponsible living. Walking out into the sunlight of Main Street from the shadows of the waterfront, I wondered if I was really alert and prepared enough for such a change. Ready or not, my journey was about to begin.

The world's transformation was before long quite obvious to me. My old friends were married already and secure in their domestic lives. Everyone appeared much too busy for the fun and easy bachelor life. I found myself alone on an island of non-stop activity. My friends were completely engrossed in fighting their own battles.

Sail Away

Being the lone bachelor amongst three brothers, I returned to my mother's home to sketch a plan for a future that I had until then for the most part ignored and neglected.

Between ocean voyages I had been seeing Chris, a San Francisco girl just out of college who was teaching kindergarten. We had courted mostly by mail when I was sailing and we would see each other when I was back in port. Before any plans for the future were finalized, I was sure of one thing—she was the girl for me!

Her father had been a sea captain and she was truly her father's girl. Brains, breeding and sophistication were all hers in a style completely lacking in superficiality. Her interest embraced the person rather than position. After all, she was putting her trust in a beginner who had built up very little security. Her cool good looks and the deepness of her dark brown eyes signaled a selfless manner she brought to the world. She was a true reason for a man to leave the sea far behind. The thought of her always brought the music in.

I had the girl and now I just had to complete the plan: a job in merchandising, a new car, an apartment overlooking the waterfront and bay, college pals of Chris's as party friends, and soon enough, a quiet wedding per-

When the Music Comes In

formed by my best friend, a schoolmate-turned-padre.

After about three years it was time to become more serious. This feeling had been waiting in the wings like a thief hiding in my closet. I thankfully embraced it in the arrival of three robust children, a house on a hilltop, and the ever-present mortgage to temper our excitement. Through it all, we had each other and the glow of the music coming in.

Life moved on to a happy beat until, as often happens in a land of constant harvests, the sun suddenly seemed to disappear much faster from the world's horizon. Children moving on to adult independence, I moved on to quiet retirement, and a fatal illness took Chris, leaving a bright world to fade.

For a few years after Chris's death, I again traveled a highway of non-responsibility and rescue from days of stress, worry, and sadness.

They are lost in the past now as memories mount. The music comes in, swelling to near-crescendo. It enlivens the drama of a life nearing finality, and will be there until the score is over and the conductor puts down his baton for the last time.

Sail Away

I have lain in the sun,
I have toil'd as I might,
I have thought as I would,
And now it is night

My bed full of sleep,
My heart of content
For friends that I met
The way that I went

For a happier lot
Than God giveth me
It never hath been
Nor ever shall be.
—Robert Bridges

Acknowledgements

This **Stillpoint/Memory** project has been made possible through the generous support of the following:

Chuck Abernathy, Craig Allen, Anonymous, Alexandra Beritzhoff, John Beritzhoff, Michael Beritzhoff, Peter Beritzhoff, Cindy, Christine Gengaro, Sarah Grant, Carol Gunby, Katie Janssen, Steve Kettmann, Catherine King, Gloria King, Chuck Lee, Diana Lee, Barb Lyon, Sandee McCready, Joy Millman, Joy Mundy, Steve Pence, Lornaa Pickrell, Vickie Rozell, Phoenix Simms, Robert Snader, Kristin Vaughn, Meredith Vecchio, Victoria Wray-Greening, Bob Weiss, Kickstarter...

and especially Lisa Beritzhoff

About Jack Beritzhoff

JACK BERITZHOFF was born in Alameda, CA in 1918. He is a fourth—generation Californian, the descendent of a California pioneer.

Jack served as a member of the United States Merchant Marine from 1942, at the height of World War II, to 1952, at the end of the Korean War.

Since leaving his life at sea on a San Francisco pier over fifty years ago, he has lived in the Bay Area town of Mill Valley. He has three children and three grandchildren. Jack started writing at the age of ninety-one.

For more information about the United States Merchant Marine, visit the service's web site, **USMM.org**

# Stillpoint Digital Press

Stillpoint Digital Press is a publisher of fine digital and print books that aims to provide digital publishing with a human face. We provide a full range of editorial services, from editing, layout and ebook conversion to distribution and marketing.

Stillpoint/Memory is one of our most exciting projects: a line of memoirs sharing the stories of people who may not be household names, but whose experiences will take your breath away. If, as Socrates said, "the unexamined life is not worth living," these are tales of lives that have not only be well worth the living, but well worth examining as well.

For more information, visit us on the web at:

StillpointDigital.com

Read these other Stillpoint titles:

- *Excursions to the Far Side of the Mind: A Book of Memes* by Howard Rheingold
- *Myths to Live By* by Joseph Campbell
- *A Joseph Campbell Companion: Reflections on the Art of Living* by Joseph Campbell
- *Sacred Precinct* by Jacqueline Kudler
- *Sexy Lexy* by Kate Moore
- *Sweet Bargain* by Kate Moore
- *The Seven Gods of Luck: A Japanese Folk Tale* retold by David Kudler, illustrated by Linda Finch

and more!

For more information, visit us on the web at

Stillpoint Digital.com

Made in the USA
Columbia, SC
04 June 2021